Animals on the Farm
Goats

Linda Aspen-Baxter
and Heather Kissock

MEDIA ENHANCED BOOKS
AV2
BY WEIGL™
ADDED VALUE • AUDIO VISUAL

www.av2books.com

Go to **www.av2books.com**, and enter this book's unique code.

BOOK CODE

H570249

AV² by Weigl brings you media enhanced books that support active learning.

AV² provides enriched content that supplements and complements this book. Weigl's AV² books strive to create inspired learning and engage young minds in a total learning experience.

Your AV² Media Enhanced books come alive with...

Audio
Listen to sections of the book read aloud.

Video
Watch informative video clips.

Embedded Weblinks
Gain additional information for research.

Try This!
Complete activities and hands-on experiments.

Key Words
Study vocabulary, and complete a matching word activity.

Quizzes
Test your knowledge.

Slide Show
View images and captions, and prepare a presentation.

... and much, much more!

Published by AV² by Weigl.
350 5th Avenue, 59th Floor
New York, NY 10118
Website: www.av2books.com   www.weigl.com

Library of Congress Cataloging-in-Publication Data

Kissock, Heather.
 Goats / Heather Kissock and Linda Aspen-Baxter.
      p. cm. -- (Animals on the farm)
 ISBN 978-1-61690-927-7 (hardcover : alk. paper) -- ISBN 978-1-61690-573-6 (online)
 1. Goats--Juvenile literature. I. Aspen-Baxter, Linda. II. Title.
 SF383.35.K57 2012
 636.3'9--dc23
                                    2011023420

Printed in the United States of America in North Mankato, Minnesota
1 2 3 4 5 6 7 8 9 0 15 14 13 12 11

062011
WEP030611

Senior Editor: Heather Kissock   Art Director: Terry Paulhus

Weigl acknowledges Getty Images as the primary image supplier for this title.

Animals on the Farm

Goats

CONTENTS

I am a small farm animal. Farmers keep me for my milk and wool.

I am a mammal. I have hair all over my body.

6

7

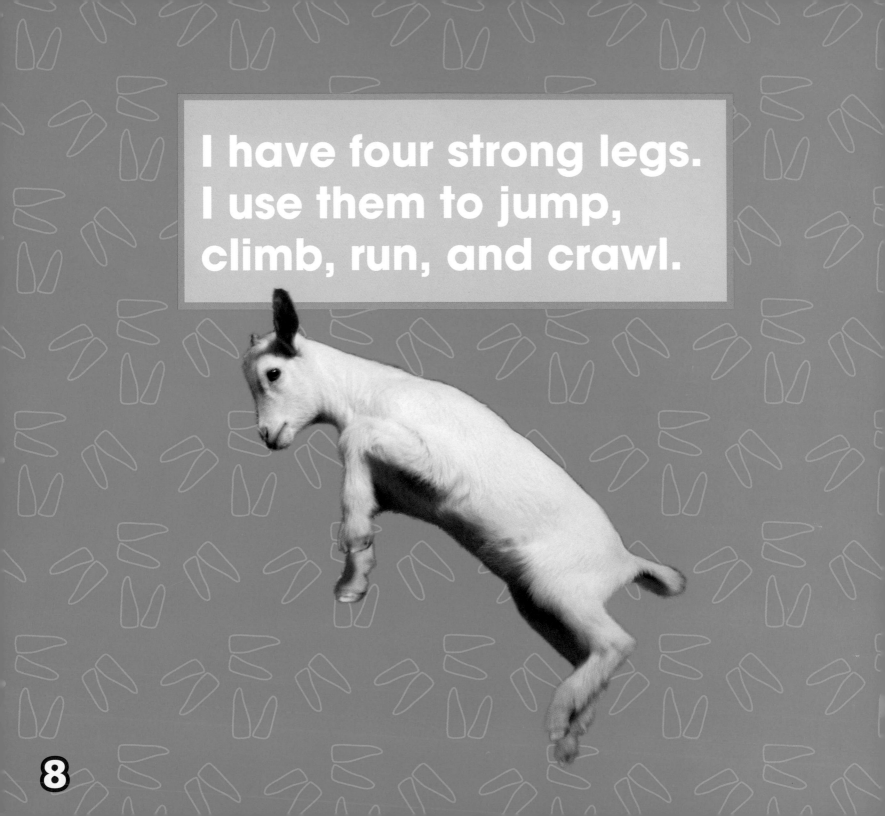

I have four strong legs.
I use them to jump,
climb, run, and crawl.

10

I grow horns on the top of my head. My horns never stop growing.

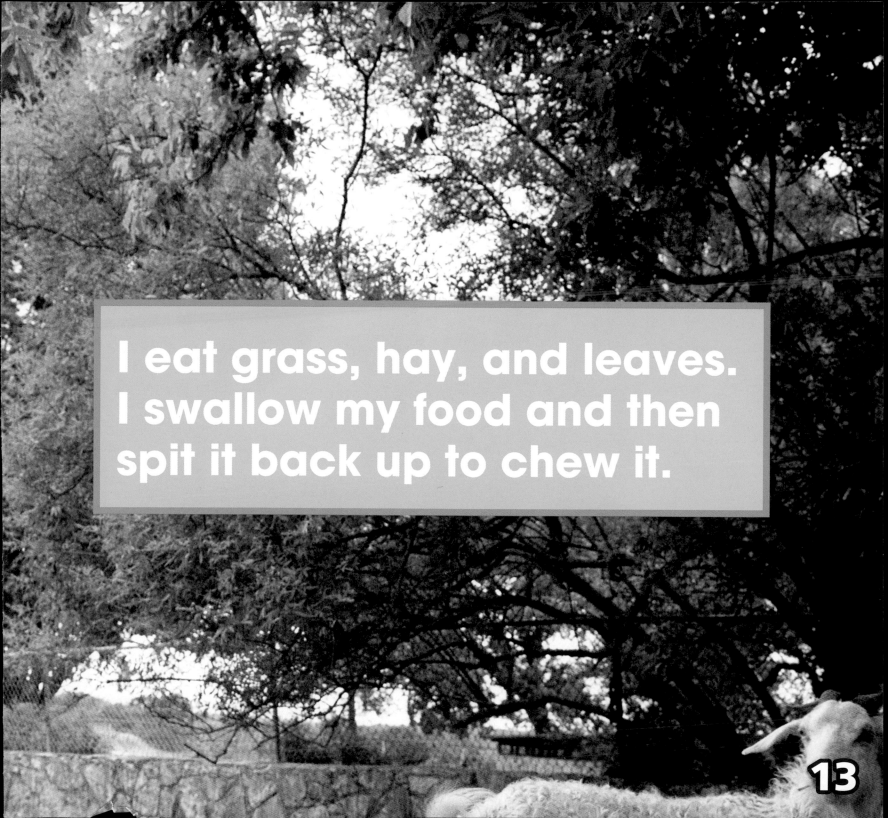

I eat grass, hay, and leaves. I swallow my food and then spit it back up to chew it.

13

How do I talk to other goats?
I "baa" at them. This is
called bleating.

I am very friendly.
I make friends
with goats and
other animals.

16

I often have babies
in the spring.

18

My babies are called kids.

My babies drink my milk. I make about 1 gallon of milk every day.

20

GOAT FACTS

This page provides more detail about the interesting facts found in the book. Simply look at the corresponding page number to match the fact.

Pages 4-5

Farmers keep goats for milk and wool. Goat milk is used in a variety of products. Besides being a beverage, goat milk is put in soap and used to make cheese. Goats can have short or long hair, which can also be curly, silky, or coarse. The hair from cashmere and angora goats is used to make sweaters and other clothing.

Pages 6–7

Goats are mammals. There are three main features that distinguish mammals from other animals. All mammals grow hair or fur all over their body. They are also warm-blooded, which means that they can produce their own body heat. As well, the females of a mammal species are able to produce milk for their young to feed on.

Pages 8–9

Goats have strong legs that they use for jumping, climbing, running, and crawling. Goats are agile and active animals. They can climb trees and jump over fences and other large objects. Their surefootedness helps them leap easily from one spot to another. Some goats can leap up to 6 feet (1.8 meters) in the air.

Pages 10–11

Goats grow horns on the top of their head. Very few goats do not have horns. A goat's horns are hollow and curve backward over the head. The horns never stop growing. Male goats have larger horns than females. Goats use their horns to butt other goats and animals that are perceived as a threat.

Pages 12–13

Goats swallow their food and then spit it back up to chew it. Goats are ruminants. They have a four-part stomach to help them break down their food. When goats chew their cud, they regurgitate feed to break it down more for digestion. As they chew, their mouths add saliva to the feed. This aids digestion.

Pages 14–15

Goats talk to other goats by bleating. Goats are typically quiet animals. They tend to bleat only when they are stressed, hungry, ill, or calling for attention. Mother goats bleat when calling to their young. They are able to recognize the bleating of their offspring.

Pages 16–17

Goats like to be with other goats and other animals. Goats are social animals. They are friendly and naturally curious. They explore new things by sniffing and nibbling. Goats are very intelligent animals. They can learn how to open the latches on pens and gates.

Pages 18–19

Goats often have babies in the spring. Their babies are called kids. Mother goats are called does or nannies. They carry their babies for about five months before they are born. When they give birth, it is called kidding. Most nannies have one or two kids at a time.

Pages 20–21

Kids drink milk that their mothers make. A nanny produces about 1 gallon (3.8 liters) of milk every day. They are weaned, or taken off the milk, when they are about 3 months old. Kids grow quickly. They are considered fully grown when they are about 30 months old.

WORD LIST

Research has shown that as much as 65 percent of all written material published in English is made up of 300 words. These 300 words cannot be taught using pictures or learned by sounding them out. They must be recognized by sight. This book contains 45 common sight words to help young readers improve their reading fluency and comprehension. This book also teaches young readers several important content words. These words are paired with pictures to aid in learning and improve understanding.

Page	Sight Words First Appearance	Page	Content Words First Appearance
4	a, and, for, I, keep, me, my, small	4	farmers, milk, wool
6	all, have, over	6	body, hair, mammal
8	four, run, them, to, use	8	legs
11	grow, head, of, on, never, stop, the	11	horns
13	back, eat, food, it, then, up	13	grass, hay, leaves
15	at, called, do, how, is, other, this	15	bleating, goats
16	animals, make, very, with	16	friends
18	in, often	18	babies
19	are	19	kids
20	about, every		

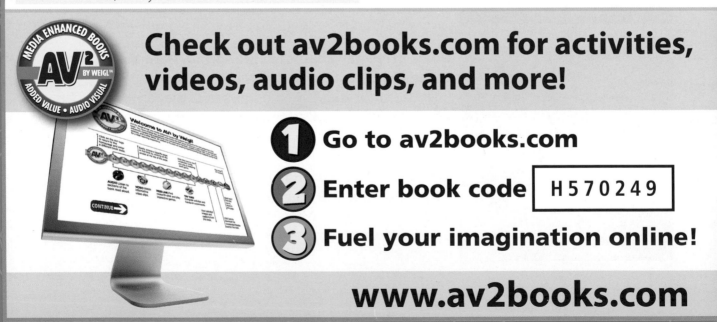